Foreword

DIVINE STRATEGIES FOR SUCCESS

Biblical Principles for Success at Life

ROB YANOK

Unless otherwise indicated, all Scripture quotations are taken from the King James Version of the Bible.

Divine Strategies for Success
(Conditioning Yourself for an Extraordinary Life)
ISBN

Published by Success@Life Publishing
P.O. Box 2635, Mansfield, Ohio, 44906

DEDICATION

This book is dedicated to my three children,

CIERRA, CHRISTIAN AND GRAYSON

You have taught me that my relationship with you
is greater than my achievements. You are my name
and legacy in this life. May the principles that I teach you
ever live within you and never be forgotten.
Being your Daddy is what makes me successful!

Table of Contents

Foreword by Dr. Dave Martin

When Robert Yanok speaks, thousands are affected.

He is trusted because of his untarnished integrity.
He is treasured for his unswerving loyalty.
He is loved for his genuine passion.
He is remembered for the unforgettable revelation he teaches.

Having sat at the feet of uncommon mentors his entire life; Robert Yanok shares practical yet powerful keys to increase the excellence and productivity of your life, business, or ministry.

Divine Strategies for Success should be required reading for anyone committed to increasing the quality of their life. The pages flow from start to finish with timeless wisdom and sound principles.

That is why this book is so important.

I have not read a more effective book on success than this book by Robert Yanok.

Dr. Dave Martin
President & CEO of Dave Martin International

Introduction

In 1952, American clergyman Norman Vincent Peale authored his best selling book entitled, "The Power of Positive Thinking." Since then motivational books, videos, cassettes, and lectures on how people can hone their potential and improve their lives have proliferated in North America. It is estimated that more than 20 million adults participate in some kind of self-help program. Their collective mission: to improve their quality of life by enhancing themselves intellectually, spiritually, socially, and physically.

For years I searched for the answers to make my life a success. *Why?*

People want to be successful. But many do not know what to do to achieve success, and those who do know will not do what they are supposed to do. Success in today's world is usually defined by the glitz and glamour of Hollywood or some overrated, flamboyant athlete that consumes his paycheck with his jewelry, car, and clothes. You may ask the question, *"What is success?"* Well, I believe it is more than what you accumulate, possess, or achieve. I believe success is a journey, not just a destination. If a person has arrived at what we call success, then we ought to be at their funeral. Success is what we become. If we are on the right path then we are on the road to success.

Over the last 13 years, I have found strategies and tools, which can immediately help individuals to change the quality of their life and get on that road to success. I've applied them myself, and I continue to apply them, and now I have the opportunity to share them with you. This will be an exciting journey that you and I can take together.

A journey towards success. On this road to success there are strategies that will keep us on that journey if you and I will follow them. The strategies that you will read about in this book are ancient and full of wisdom, but still very relevant for our time.

"This Book of the law shall not depart out of thy mouth;
but thou shalt meditate therein day and night,
that thou mayest observe to do according to all
that is written therein: for then thou shalt make thy way
prosperous, and then thou shalt have good success."

— JOSHUA 1:8

Success Secret 1

The Source of Success

Imagine being able to sit down and have conversations with the most successful men and women in the world. Successful people in wealth and riches, happiness, and fulfillment. Imagine listening to their secrets, their strategies on how they achieved success; learning from their wisdom, experiences and knowledge. You would be able to gain valuable insights into the Divine Strategies for Success. But you don't have to imagine anymore. You are able to do just that. You can see and read the conversations that these folks had to bring them to the level of success. You will see success in its proper perspective. Not success as you have heard about it before or seen it on television. But true success for every person who desires it. Is that your desire? If so, you can achieve what you desire. Yes, you can! It is not based upon your past. It is not based upon your social or financial status. You can start today by applying these divine strategies to every aspect of your life.

By now you are probably wondering where these strategies come from. Where are the divine strategies for ultimate success in my life, family, finances, and business? Well, my dear friend, the ancient wisdom for relevant times today comes from the world's oldest and best selling book. The strategies in this book are 6000 years old, and the most successful and prominent people on this planet have used them. By applying them to their lives, they have achieved the success that they desired. I believe that after you encounter these strategies for success you too will never be the same. This book has been the number one best seller since the inception of the printing press, which was invented for the initial purpose of reproducing it. The truths in this book are ancient wisdom, but you will receive a fresh, new practical way to understand them and apply these powerful strategies to your life to achieve success.

There are a lot of books out on the market today that give you techniques or methods for success. In the remainder of this book, I want to give you principles. You see techniques and methods change, but principles never change. They are eternal. Therefore, that is the purpose of writing this book. The principles that you and I need to know about success, wealth, and happiness are contained within the binding of one book, the Bible.

The principles that you and I need to know about success, wealth, and happiness are contained within the binding of one book, the Bible.

The Bible's principles have withstood all the tests of time. Within its pages you will find the answer to all of life's problems and opportunities. Napoleon Bonaparte said, "The Bible is no mere book, but a Living Creature, with a power that conquers all who oppose it." If you take the message of the Bible, success will leap from the written pages and become a total reality in your life. The only request it will ask of you concerning its strategies is that you will hear, believe, and do what it says! In the Old Testament book of Isaiah, the ancient script declared that, "If you will be willing and obedient, you shall eat the good of the land." If we will be willing to hear what the Bible says concerning success, then be obedient concerning its principles, the by product will be the good of the land. In other words, Success! There is always a prerequisite to success, a price that needs to be paid. If you are willing to pay that price you will reap its reward.

God's Word is the greatest book ever written. In it God Himself speaks to men. It is a book of divine instruction. It offers comfort in sorrow, guidance in perplexity, advice for our problems, rebuke for our sins, and daily inspiration for our every need.

The Word of God is not simply one book. It is an entire library of books covering the whole range of literature. It includes history, prophecy, poetry, drama, biography, philosophy, science, and a wealth of inspiration for our life. All or part of the Bible has been translated into more than 1,200 languages, and every year more copies of the Bible are sold than any other single book.

The Bible alone truly answers the greatest questions that men of all ages have asked: "Where have I come from?" "Where am I going?" "Why am I here?" "How can I know Truth?" For the Word of God reveals the truth about God, explains the origin of man, points out the only way of salvation and eternal life, and explains the age-old problem of sin and suffering. It gives us total direction on how to live our life. We are to live by faith, live by God's Word.

The Word of God is what will endure forever. Psalm 119:89 says, "Forever, O Lord, thy word is settled in heaven." You see, God's Word is settled in heaven. The word "settled" is the Hebrew word "natsav" which means "to set up, be stationed, stand, to be firmed, be healthy, to set place, establish boundaries, position of authority." The word gives us that foundation. When you stand on the Word you become unmovable. Isaiah 40:8 declares, "The grass withereth, the flower fadeth: but the word of our God shall stand forever." Matthew 5:18, "For verily I say unto you, till heaven and earth pass, one jot or tittle shall in no wise pass from the law, till all be fulfilled." Matthew 24:35, "Heaven and earth shall pass away, but my words shall not pass away." The Word of God, its existence, is forever.

The Bible is not just a book. It is a God-breathed, God-indwelt, God-inspired message. We are to believe only what the Word of God says, not what we think it says or what someone else says that it says.

II Peter 1:21, "*For the prophecy came not in old time by the will of man: but holy men of God spake as they were moved by the Holy Ghost.*"

We must have discipline to study God's Word and put it on the inside of our spirit man. II Timothy 2:15-16 says, *"Study to show thyself approved unto God, a workman that needeth not to be ashamed, rightly dividing the word of truth. But shun profane babblings: for they will increase unto more ungodliness."* When you begin to study God's Word it brings God's approval on your life and it puts you in agreement with God.

The Word of God has integrity. It means what is says and does what it says. Hebrews 4:12 in the Phillips Translation says, "*For the Word that God speaks is alive and active...*" In the New Living Translation, *"For whatever God says to us is full of living power. Sharper than the sharpest knife, cutting deep into our innermost thoughts and desires, it exposes us for what we really are."* Pretty simple. That my dear friend is how powerful God's Word is. The Word of God is powerful because God is powerful. God and His Word are the same (John 1:1-5). Integrity is when the Word backs up the man and the man is a man of his word. Integrity produces power, trust and honor. Some may trust in horses, some may trust in chariots, but we will put our trust in the Lord. Proverbs 3 declares that we are to, "Trust in the Lord with all of our heart, lean not to our own understanding. In all of your ways acknowledge him and he shall direct your path." We can put our trust in God, because he backs up His Word.

We are born again by the Word of God. I Peter 1:23-25 states, *"Being born again, not of corruptible seed, but of incorruptible, by the Word of God, which liveth and abideth forever. For all flesh is as grass, and all the glory of man as the flower of grass. The grass withereth, and the flower thereof falleth away: but theWord of the Lord endureth forever. And this is the word which by the gospel is preached unto you."* You see the word "liveth" is the Greek word "zao" meaning "to have life, be alive or used of natural living." The Word of God brings life. The word "abideth" is the Greek word "meno" which means, "to remain, dwell, or abide, to endure, and to last." Folks, all you and I have to do is hold on to God's Word concerning any circumstance. That is what will abide. Not our problem. God's Word.

Without the Word of God we cannot even be born again; because we are born again by the Word of God. It is the seed. That is how powerful God's Word is. When the Word of God is preached and it is heard, that seed is planted into the heart of the hearer, which produces salvation. James 1:21 says, "...and receive with meekness the engrafted word, which is able to save your souls." The word "meekness" does not mean weakness, it actually is defined as teachable. Now the word "engrafted" means to implant. When we are teachable we receive the "implanted" word, meaning that the Word of God is implanted into our hearts, and it saves our souls (mind, will and emotions).

You will never achieve your potential in the Word of God unless you are persuaded of the importance of reading the Word habitually on a continual basis. In Luke 4, verse 16, "And he came to Nazereth, where he had been brought up: As His custom was, He went into the synagogue on the Sabbath, and He stood up for to read." The secret to your spiritual advancement is hidden in your daily routine. Reading and studying the Word strengthens your faith. Like food for your body is necessary on a regular basis, the Word of God is spirit food and mind food. You may not sense its effect upon you immediately. But the full impact of exposing your thinking to God's Word is progressive.

The problem with most people is that they feed their bodies three meals a day, but they feed their spirit and soul one snack a week. Feeding our spirit and soul is just as important as feeding our natural bodies. Could you just imagine what we would be like spiritually if we fed our spirit and soul on a continual basis as much as we feed our bodies? Take the Word and do what Jeremiah did, he ate the Word. Jeremiah 15:16, "Thy words were found and I did eat them..." Eat it. Just eat it. Get full of the Word of God. Reading the Word is eating the Word. Don't just read it religiously, read it out of a relationship with God. When you get into the Word, the Word will get into you. The by-product...SUCCESS.

YOUR SUCCESS IS IN YOUR MOUTH

The principles that spiritual success are based on are spiritual laws. They will work for whosoever will apply these laws. Therefore, confession is not a theory, it is a spiritual law. You see, possessing success comes by confessing success.

"When Jesus came into the coasts of Caesarea Philippi, He asked his disciples, saying, Whom do men say that I the Son of man am? And they said, Some say that thou art John the Baptist: some, Elias; and others Jeremias, or one of the prophets. He saith unto them, But who say ye that I am? And Simon Peter answered and said, Thou art the Christ, the Son of the living God. And Jesus answered and said unto him, Blessed art thou, Simon Barjona: for flesh and blood hath not revealed it unto thee, but my Father which is in heaven. And I say also unto thee, That thou art Peter, and upon this rock I will build my church; and the gates of hell shall not prevail against it. And I will give unto thee the KEYS of the kingdom of heaven; and whatsoever thou shalt bind on earth shall be bound in heaven: and whatsoever thou shalt loose on earth shall be loosed in heaven"

— MATTHEW 16:13-19

Satan is a spiritual fugitive, a criminal running from justice. In Luke 10:18, Jesus beheld Satan as lightning falling from heaven. The scripture declares also, that "the earth is the Lord's and the fullness thereof." The earth is a prison for Satan and his demon spirits.

Adam was the warden of this prison until he sinned and lost the keys to Satan. But, Jesus got them back when He died and on the third day He rose again. Now we have the KEYS!

We have the keys to keep Satan and his negative influences in prison and to unlock people out of prison. We are not supposed to be in prison or bondage. The devil is, but he keeps getting out! So God has given us Keys to lock and unlock. It is time that we walk in the authority that God has given us to use the keys and exercise dominion on the earth.

REVELATION GETS THE KEYS

Revelation does not change the Word of God. It just lets you in on what the Word of God says. It reveals what's already there!

Jesus is asking us all the inevitable question, "Whom say ye that I am?" You see, if you are going to be a disciple, you cannot parrot what others say about him, you must know Jesus for yourself and have a revelation. When you can tell Jesus who He is, He'll turn around and tell you who you are. That is revelation knowledge. The power of God flows through those who have revelation, not theory or information.

Information is intellectual knowledge about something. Today we no longer want convictions in our lives, we want decisions. A decision for Jesus is intellectual. Conversion is spiritual. If someone can talk you into being saved, then someone can talk you out of being saved. Let me tell you what people can't take from you — that what you experienced for yourself! Jesus asked, who do men say that I am? They in turn said, "some say..." That, my friend, is intellectual. Information comes from what some say. But revelation comes from what God says.

KEYS = AUTHORITY

Having keys means you have authority. God won't give anyone keys to this vehicle unless they first know how to drive. That comes by revelation, which is instruction by the Holy Spirit.

Ecclesiastes 8:4 declares, *"Where the word of a King is there is power."* The word of a King has authority. His word was never questioned and it was always carried out. We are Kings and Priests unto God, A Royal Priesthood. Our vocabulary has power beyond the natural realm into the spirit realm.

How do we use this authority (or keys?) The root word for authority is "author," which means, "one who works with WORDS." My friend, we trigger our authority (turn the keys) when we speak! Our confession releases the power of God.

Ephesians 5:1 states, *"Be ye therefore followers (imitators) of God, as dear children."* In imitating or following God we need to understand His dialogue. Jesus said I only say what my father tells me to say. Obviously, the father is saying things or has said things that we need to say and speak. We are His children, His sons and daughters. We need to be like our Dad.

In Hebrews, the writer penned, *"Through faith we understand that the worlds were framed by the word of God..."* In the Amplified Version framed means fashioned, put in order and equipped for their intended purpose or use. We don't need to recreate THE WORLD, but we do need to recreate OUR WORLD, or our situation.

God's Word is creative power. When God spoke in the beginning, He spoke to darkness and brought forth light. His word created. Words transmit. The Word of God is not void of power, we are just void of the Word of God.

FAITH AND CONFESSION

Jesus said in Mark 11:22, *"Have faith in God."* The original text states, *"Have the faith of God."* Therefore our faith must be "in

God." Faith is not a trick formed with our words. Faith is the spoken expression of our hearts. As the late Dr. Lester Sumrall said, "Faith is simply knowing God."

Jesus goes on to say in verse 23, *"For verily I SAY unto you, That whosoever shall SAY unto this mountain, be thou removed, and be thou cast into the sea; and shall not doubt in his heart, but shall BELIEVE that those things which he SAITH shall come to pass; he shall have whatsoever he SAITH."*

Confession is not a formula for getting things from God. It is not a theory; it is a spiritual law. In this verse of scripture, Jesus outlines the demonstration for our authority over the enemy. If you will notice, Jesus tells us to believe once but he tells us three times to "say." Our problem today in the church is not believing. Everyone "believes." You cannot be saved without believing. Believing is what gets us to this point of even reading the Word. The problem is not with believing; it is with our "saying."

To be saved we must speak the right thing. Romans 10:9-10, *"That if thou shalt CONFESS with thy MOUTH the Lord Jesus, and shalt believe in thine heart that God raised Jesus from the dead, thou shalt be saved. For with the heart man believeth unto righteousness; and with the MOUTH CONFESSION is made unto SALVATION."* Therefore, our lips need to begin to speak the right things, namely the Word of God.

THE WORD

Death and life are in the power of the tongue. By thy words thou shalt be justified and by thy words thou shalt be condemned. The tongue of the wise is health. And a man shall eat good by the fruit of his mouth.

The statement that we have heard and said throughout the years has been accepted and confessed, and I believe repented of: "Sticks and stones may break my bones, but words will never hurt me." My friend, that is WRONG! Words can kill you. The Word of God says,

"Death and Life are in the power of the tongue." If you don't know what you're doing with your words, they will destroy you.

"The integrity of the upright shall guide them: but the PERVERSENESS of transgressors shall destroy them."
— PROVERBS 11:3

The word *perverseness* means crooked and contrary speech.

"A wholesome tongue is a tree of life: but perverseness therein is a breach in the spirit."
— PROVERBS 15:4

"Put away from thee a froward mouth (false and dishonest speech) and perverse lips put far from thee."
— PROVERBS 4:24

"He that hath a froward heart findeth no good: and he that hath a perverse tongue falleth into mischief."
— PROVERBS 17:20

"..he that is perverse in his lips, is a fool."
— PROVERBS 19:1

The words of your mouth feed your spirit. You are what you eat! Luke 6:45 says, *"A good man out of the good treasure of his heart bringeth forth that which is good; and an evil man out of the evil treasure of his heart bringeth forth that which is evil: for out of the abundance of the heart the mouth speaketh."* Garbage in, garbage out! Jesus said it is not what goes into a man that defileth him, it is what comes out of him. The defilement doesn't happen until we let what comes in, go out! Therefore we must watch what comes into our spirit. So quit saying what you've been saying. James said to be slow to speak.

If you and I will change our thinking, we will change our speaking. Ephesians says let no corrupt communication come out of your mouth. Corrupt is anything that doesn't line up with what God says about a situation. Philippians 2:5 declares, *"Let this mind be in you, which was also in Christ Jesus."* Now if you want to know what to think, memorize Philippians 4:7-8.

CONFESSION DETERMINES THE POSSESSION

"For verily I say unto you, that whosoever shall say unto this mountain, be thou removed, and be thou cast into the sea; and shall not doubt in his heart, but shall believe that those things which he saith shall come to pass; he shall have whatsoever he saith."
— MARK 11:23

What we are going to learn about in this chapter is that our words dominate our lives. They determine our destiny. Our confession shows us what we really believe in our hearts. You see, the words that we release from our mouth will determine what we possess in this life. Our destiny actually hangs on our confession, whether it be negative or positive. In other words, our confession determines our possession. We will evaluate this in the book of Numbers concerning the 12 spies and the report they were to bring back to the children of Israel. Their confession determined their possession.

"And the Lord SPAKE unto Moses saying, Send thou men that they may search the land of Canaan, which I give unto the children of Israel: of every tribe of their fathers shall ye send a man, everyone a ruler among them. And Moses by the commandment of the Lord sent them from the wilderness of Paran: all those men were heads of the children of Israel." Numbers 13:1-3

First of all, the Lord spoke to Moses and told him to send out men to search the land that HE GAVE to the children of Israel. God had already given the land to them. So they were to go into their own land and search it out. The land already belonged to them. All they needed to do was get familiar with their own land.

When we were born again we were enlisted into God's army. He promised us that wherever our feet shall walk, that ground is ours to take. We have authority as a believer in the realm of the spirit. Jesus said, "Behold I give you ALL POWER over the enemy. Greater is he that is in you than he that is in the world." He gave us power after the

Holy Spirit came upon us. We have the authority within us as a believer. What God is calling us to do is to demonstrate our authority. *How?* By the words that we speak.

To access the spirit realm you must walk in the spirit. The spirit realm is a place that a lot of believers don't go into because they don't understand it. Most believers live either in the flesh realm or the soulish realm, which is the mind, will, and emotions. The natural mind does not receive the things of the spirit for they are foolishness to him. You can't figure out spiritual things with your natural mind. IMPOSSIBLE! You understand it by faith. The spirit realm is the real realm and in that realm we have authority. The words we release from our lips in the natural are first manifested in the spiritual. Proverbs declares, "Death and Life are in the power of the tongue." Spiritual death and life and natural death and life are all in the power (authority) of the tongue.

The wilderness of Paran is Kadesh Barnea. It means a desert of a fugitive. It was often a place of defeat, failure, and death for the nation of Israel. You see their destination was determined by their confession.

EVIL REPORT

The story in detail is found in Numbers chapter 13. There were two types of confession released by the 12 spies. The ten spies' confession was a negative one. The word that they brought back was, "we are not able to go up against the people; for they are stronger than we. They are men of great stature. And we saw the giants and we were in OUR own sight as grasshoppers and so we were in their sight."

The scripture says in verse 32 that they brought up an EVIL REPORT. God says an evil report is one of doubt and unbelief. Notice that their perception of themselves was based on their evil report. That is why you need to speak the Word of God over your life everyday. Don't look at yourself in the natural; speak and confess what is in the spirit. Smith Wigglesworth used to say, "I am a 1000 times bigger on the inside (my spirit) than I am on the outside." You see the word he confessed spoke what he really was.

When you speak words of doubt and unbelief to people, you are speaking an evil report. Speaking words of doubt and unbelief is rebelling against God. Why? God has already given us promises in His Word. Psalm 138:2, "...for thou hast magnified thy word above thy name." Hebrews 1:3, "...He upholds all things by HIS WORD..." You can read in Deuteronomy 28:1-14 about His promises. Therefore when you speak words of doubt and unbelief, you are actually telling God He is a liar and His promises aren't true! Before they ever spied out the land God had already told them that it belonged to them.

The ten spies got exactly what they said. They possessed what they confessed. They said, "We can't do it", and guess what; "they did not do it!" They wandered in the wilderness until every man 20 years old and older died!

WORDS ARE CONTAGIOUS

If you will notice what the ten spies spoke, the people also spoke:

"And all the children of Israel murmured against Moses and against Aaron: and the whole congregation said unto them, Would God that we had died in the land of Egypt! or would God we had died in this wilderness!"
— NUMBERS 14:2

My friend, that is exactly what they got. Their confession determined their possession. They died in the wilderness. Even in verse 4 it says, "they said one to another..." My friend, think before you speak. The words that come out of your mouth from your spirit have death and life. They are contagious and what you speak others will also speak.

That is what happened while the people were building the tower of Babel when the whole earth was of one language and one speech. Notice in Genesis 11:3, they said one to another, "Let us make brick and build a city and tower whose top may reach heaven." Their purpose was prideful, to make a name for themselves, and God said nothing will be restrained from them. The place was called Babel, because God confounded their language (confession). He changed their speech.

Faith is always expressed in words. What you say is what your faith is speaking. The words you speak indicate what you believe in your heart and ultimately determine what you will receive in life. We often create our own negative situations ourselves with our wrong believing, wrong thinking, and wrong speaking.

Joshua and Caleb got exactly what they said. They confessed and said, "let us go up at once, and possess it; for we are well able to overcome it." At 85 years old, Caleb proclaimed in the promised land, "Give me this mountain." They confessed and they possessed.

WHAT CONFESSION ACCOMPLISHES

1. Confession reveals what we really believe in our heart.

a. Joshua and Caleb operated by faith and they compared the giants not to them, but to the Almighty God!

b. Luke 6:45 *"A good man out of the good treasure of his heart bringeth forth that which is good; and an evil man out of the evil treasure of his heart bringeth forth that which is evil; For out of the abundance of the heart his mouth speaketh."*

2. Your words set the boundaries of your life. You will never receive anything from God beyond the words you speak.

a. The ten spies and Israelites never went any further than the words of doubt and unbelief they spoke. That is why there was no promise land for them.

b. Joshua and Caleb's words fixed their boundaries. They said, "we are well able to possess the land." And they did! Faith and confession does not control God, it just pulls that which is in the spirit realm into the natural to benefit the kingdom.

3. The words you speak affect your spirit, soul and body!

a. "Pleasant words are as an honeycomb, sweet to the soul, and health to the bones." Proverbs 16:24.

b. "If you don't bridle your tongue, you deceive your own heart (spirit)." James 1:26

THE SWORD OF THE SPIRIT

"And hath made my mouth like a sharp sword;
in the shadow of His hand hath He hid me, and made me
a polished shaft; in His quiver He hid me;"
— ISAIAH 49:2

"And take the helmet of salvation, and the
sword of the spirit, which is the Word of God."
— EPHESIANS 6:17

HOW NEGATIVE THOUGHTS COME

In II Corinthians 2:11, the scripture says, *"Lest Satan should get an advantage of us; we are not ignorant of his devices."* II Corinthians 10:5 declares, *"Casting down imaginations and every high thing that exalts itself against the knowledge of God, and bringing into captivity every thought to the obedience of Christ."* The word for devices in Greek is the same word for thoughts. So Satan's devices are the thoughts that he puts in our minds. Thoughts are words put into pictures in our mind. Therefore, you combat Satan's thoughts with God's thoughts, which is the Word of God. Releasing that word is confessing that word.

First of all, to speak God's Word, we must eat God's Word. Jeremiah said, *"Thy words were found and I did eat them...."* Luke said what is in your heart comes out of your heart when you speak, whether it be good or evil. Read Matthew 15:10-20. Jesus talks about what comes out of a man is what defiles him. Therefore, we must be eating the right thing, to speak the right thing.

Second, speaking the Word of God is a powerful instrument. *"For the word of God is quick (living) and powerful, and sharper than any two-edged sword, piercing even to the dividing asunder of soul and spirit and of the joints and marrow and is a discerner of the thoughts (devices) and intents of the heart,"* Hebrews 4:12.

Matthew 4:4 states that, *"man shall not live by bread alone, but by every word that proceedeth out of the mouth of God...."* That is not what is known as the logos word, which is the expression of thought, a message, a discourse, the Bible in its entirety, but it is the rhema word, that which is said or spoken, an utterance. Logos is the Bible as a whole and Rhema is the verse spoken. We must begin to speak the rhema word of God. It is the rhema that gives us faith (Romans 10:17). It is the rhema that heals our land. We need to hear the rhema and speak the rhema. Don't misunderstand me, we need to hear the logos word and teach the logos word. We must speak God's word to our situation. Stop talking about your problems and start talking to them. (Example: David and Goliath, He spoke to Goliath, I Samuel 17) Swing the sword of the Spirit!

A few years ago, my wife and daughter and I were traveling to our then home in Appleton, Wisconsin after ministering in South Bend, Indiana. It was around 2:00am and my wife was driving and I was sleeping. Our usual route was to go through Milwaukee, Wisconsin taking 41 North to Appleton. It is simple. But for some reason that night she did not remember or decided to try a different route back home. To this day, I still do not know where we were or what road we were on. The problem was that we were lost and we had completely run out of gas. I mean completely out! Not even a fume.

She had woken me earlier and told me that we were running out of gas and so my instruction was to find a gas station and fill up. The problem was that we could not find one. Our Nissan Sentra Sport Coupe choked along and finally went as far as it could go. And yes, you guessed it. It was done.

We pulled over and all we could see was land, cows, and a little farmhouse in the distance. Let me remind you, it was 2:00am. Needless to say, she began to cry and I got angry. Why? Well, why couldn't we go the usual way. Our daughter Cierra was 18 months old and she was sound asleep. She was not worried about anything. You're saying, yeah, she is a baby, it's 2:00a.m. God was getting ready to show us something big. He was going to show me what faith was. Not what I thought it was. Not what I was taught, but what the reality of faith really was. Hang on with me now, it gets much better.

As I opened the car door and got out, my mind was racing with what we were going to do. Oh, did I tell you that it was 10 degrees and snowing! My wife then got out and tearily asked me what we were going to do. With a frustrated and quick answer, I responded, "I don't know, just let me think!" As I said that, the Holy Spirit spoke to me and said, "Aren't you a man of Faith?" It startled me. In my carnality I wanted to say, yes, in a church service. You know what I mean. It is so easy to have faith during a great time of praise and worship and when you are surrounded by other believers, but what about when you're not there and no one is around. That is when you need the faith.

I responded, "Yes, Lord!" Then He said, "Faith is what you need." The Lord continued to let me know that He could respond to my need but it was not my need that moves Him, it was my faith. He then instructed me to activate my faith and put it into action and everything would be all right. But this great man of faith had a question...How? It is funny how I instructed people in the Word but in a time of need I didn't know what to do. The Lord and I were in a conversation outside in 10 degree, snowy weather in the middle of Wisconsin dairy land with no gas in our vehicle. Thank God he gave me the answer – His Word, which we will discuss in detail in a little bit.

His Word. He told me to quote His Word. My wife and I laid hands on our car and we prayed the prayer of faith that it would get us to where we needed to go. We got into the car and I began to quote God's Word. We then began to drive 1 mile, 2 miles, 10 miles, 13 miles, 15 miles, 17 miles, 18 miles....remember, with no gas in our car. All we had was faith and God's Word. While driving and speaking the Word of Faith, God then said turn right. As I looked ahead I saw a dirt road between two cornfields. Now let's face it. Why would I want to turn there? I don't know but that is what God said. So guess what I did? You're right. I turned right. My wife said what are you doing and where are you going? I said, I don't know, God said to turn right. As we drove down this dirt road for one mile, we looked and we were completely amazed. Because between two cornfields on a dirt road was the biggest lit up "Shell" gas station I had ever seen. We pulled in thanking God and rejoicing. We were so excited that we didn't even recognize that no one was even there getting gas. But as I filled up our tank I just looked around and gave thanks to God, but still thought it was odd that this gas station would be in the middle of two cornfields on a dirt road. As I walked in the station and headed to the pop section to get a Mountain Dew, I noticed that there was no one in the store. But when I turned around there was a man with blue jeans, plaid shirt, blonde hair, blonde mustache and blue eyes sitting on top of the counter with his elbow on the cash register. He startled me because I didn't see him when I walked in. I said hello and he said to me, "You've had car problems haven't you?" I said, "Yes, we ran out of gas." He looked at me with this fatherly smile and said, "Yes, I know! That is why we are here! Have a nice evening!" And he sent me on my way.

By faith, He let my car go 19 miles with no gas and then made a gas station in the middle of two cornfields on a dirt road

Well, needless to say, I knew what had happened and tears of excitement and joy began to stream down my face. As I approached our vehicle, my wife asked me what was the matter. I said, "That is not there," (meaning the gas station) and I began to explain to her that God had placed it there for us and provided an angel to speak to me. Folks, with God all things are possible! By faith, he let my car go 19 miles with no gas and then made a gas station in the middle of two cornfields on a dirt road and placed an angel in there to talk to me. How? By Faith! God's Word is true and it is real. The story I just told is absolutely true and in this book I will give you principles of God's Word concerning living by faith. You are able to live in a realm of supernatural faith, all the time!

THE HEBREW ASPECT OF SPEAKING THE WORD

In David Bloomgren's manual, *Prophetic Gatherings in the Local Church,* he states "... in Hebrew thought there was a casual relationship between the word spoken and the subsequent event following at it's own appointed time." Speaking the Word of the

Lord was regarded as a living entity, containing within itself divine power to accomplish itself. That Word of the Lord released a power to perform or to bring about its content. It has power. The Hebrew word for "word" is *"dabar"*, which means action or deed. Jeremiah 1:9, *"And the lord said unto me, Behold I have put my words (dabar) in thy mouth."* Dabar carries a connotation of dynamic action. To be behind and drive forward or to drive forward of that which is behind. You see Hebrew verbs always express movement or activity. The dabar word will get behind that thing which is in your way and drive it forward--sickness, disease, deliverance, etc.

Isaiah 55:11, *"So shall my word be that goeth forth out of my mouth: it shall not return unto me void, but it shall accomplish that which I please, and it shall prosper in the thing where to I sent it."* Peter said, *"If any man speak let him speak as the oracles of God."* We need to speak the Word of the Lord. Speak like God would speak. And that is releasing his Word over a situation.

A perfect example of this is found in Judges 6 and 7, the fascinating story of Gideon. Gideon was up to fight the Midianites. He was down to 300 hundred men and the Midianites were so many you couldn't even number them. But victory was going to be for Gideon. The plan was to blow their trumpets and break pitchers and hold their lamps in their left hand and the trumpet in their right and blow and CRY, "The sword of the Lord and of Gideon." When Gideon's army spoke God's Word (the sword of the Lord) against the enemy, the Midianites ran, cried, and fled and all of them turned their swords on each other and killed one another. The Word of the Lord spoken will destroy those things which come against you in the spirit.

You cannot just whisper the Word, you must proclaim the Word of God with **BOLDNESS** and **AUTHORITY** from your lips. What God is wanting in this hour is the Church to begin to walk in the realm of authority and demonstrate it by the words we confess. Our words can accomplish the destruction of Satan's kingdom and the establishing of God's Kingdom.

Never underestimate the power of God's Word spoken! Remember, God's Word is not void of power, we are just void of God's Word.

FAITH: THE RAW MATERIAL OF SUCCESS

"Faith tales God without any ifs. If God says anything, faith says, "I believe it"; faith says, "Amen" to it".
- DL Moody

Faith is the basis of manifesting God's Word to work in our life to do what it says it is going to do. Understanding faith is not complicated. Faith is not a movement. Faith is not a denomination. Faith is not a theory. Faith is a fixation on the eternal laws of God. Our faith is not based upon sense knowledge or understanding, but God's Word.

You see, the universe operates by the laws of God. The sun never rises in the north and sets in the south. It always rises in the east and sets in the west. Gravity always works. It never goes on vacation. The earth continues to rotate on its axis — it never stops. God has fixed laws that will never change. Faith is one of those laws.

Faith is a substance, a spiritual force. Kenneth Hagin says that "faith is grasping the unrealities of hope and bringing them into the realm of reality." A key verse in the chapter of faith is the familiar verse found in Hebrews 11:1, *"Now faith is the substance of things hoped for, the evidence of things not seen."* In other words, faith is based upon the promise of God's Word that I am standing on concerning my problem. The word "substance" is derived from the Greek word, *hupo stasis,* meaning to stand by something, foundation, or to be placed. Basically having the attitude of "grabbing a hold and not letting go." Faith comes from everything that the Word of God says. Faith and God's Word are the same. The Word of God and belief in that Word is what faith actually is. When you have faith in God you will have faith in His Word. God and His Word cannot be separated. Why? Because John's discourse in John 1:1 says that *"In the beginning was the word and the word was with God and the word was God."*

Therefore, to understand what faith is, we must understand how powerful God's Word is. "*For the Word of God is quick, and powerful, and sharper than any two-edged sword, piercing even to the dividing asunder of soul and spirit, and of the joints and marrow, and is a discerner of the thoughts and intent of the heart,*" Hebrews 4:12. The Living Bible says it this way, *"For whatever God says is full of living power."*

God's Word is so powerful, my friend, that He framed the inner image of the universe with His Words, then released the words filled with faith. The power in the words brought into manifestation the picture the words painted. God's Word is something that you can count on, even when everything else lets you down.

The Bible is not just a book; it is a God-breathed, God-indwelt, God-inspired message. We are to believe only what God's Word says, not what we think it says or what someone else says that it says. We are to live by faith. Live by the Word of God.

Therefore to live in the supernatural realm of faith, we must understand what faith is. And in the remaining part of this book, we will know what faith is and how to live by faith. Romans 4:17 says that *"...Faith is calling those things which be not as though they are...."* You see, your situation says one thing, but God's Word says another. To live by faith, you must not look at your problem, but look at the answer. That answer is found in God's Word. When you walk by faith, you don't walk by the circumstances of life, you walk by God's Word.

So, what is faith? Hebrews 11:1 says, *"Now faith is the substance of things hoped for, the evidence of things not seen."* The key words here to understand faith are **NOW**, **SUBSTANCE**, and **EVIDENCE**.

Faith is *now*. Faith is not yesterday or tomorrow. Faith is now. It is now faith. But how does it apply? You see, God does not operate in time. He operates in eternity. God is not bound by time. He lives in the spirit. Why? Because God is spirit (John 4:24). The spirit transcends time. The spirit is eternity. When you activate your faith you actually pull what is in eternity into your now. The Bible is not mere words; it is life and power. Even though it was written thousands of years ago, it transcends time and space and it works for us today.

That is why Jesus said, *"Heaven and earth shall pass away, but my word will abide forever."* Jesus said also, *"I am the same yesterday, today, and forever."* My friend, whatever your need is, faith gets to you. You are not going to be healed, you are healed. Why? Healing has already taken place. "By his stripes ye WERE healed." Therefore, take what has already happened on the cross, have faith, pull it out of eternity into the now and receive your healing.

Faith is the substance of things. What kind of things? Things you need! My friend, that means physical and spiritual things. Before you can ever get anything from God, you must have faith. Why? Because faith is the substance; it is the material. Creflo Dollar says it is the "stuff". You see faith is the substance for the healing you need. Faith is the substance of the house you want. Faith is the substance for your bills to be paid.

The answer is the evidence and the evidence is Faith and faith is God's Word. Evidence is the proof. You see, you don't need faith for what you have or what you can see; you need faith for what you don't have and don't see. All the evidence for what we need is found in God's Word.

God has a way to get your needs met and problems solved. The answer: Faith. Faith occurs when we quit trying to do something ourselves and we begin to trust God. Our walk with God begins with faith. It is not just something we have, it must be something God can do. Instead of talking about problems, let's talk to them. We need to have an atmosphere for faith to work. Faith will not work when there is wrong seeing, wrong believing, wrong saying, and wrong thinking. The way you see is a direct result of the way you think; the way you think is the way you believe; and the way you believe determines what you say!

"My son, attend to my words; incline thine ear to my sayings. Let them not depart from thine EYES; keep them in the midst of thine heart. For they are life unto those that find them and health to all their flesh. Keep thy heart with all diligence; for out of it are the issues of life. Put away from thee a froward mouth, and perverse lips put far from thee. Let thine EYES look right on, and let thine eyelids look straight before thee. Ponder the path of thy feet, and let all thy ways be established. Turn not to the right hand nor to the left: remove thy foot from evil."
— PROVERBS 4:20-27

Solomon is telling us to attend to his words. Whose words? God's Words. Attend to them. Incline your ear to his sayings. Then he goes on to say, "let them not depart from thine EYES; keep them in the midst of thine heart." The eyes are the gateway to the soul. What you see goes to your spirit and your heart. He goes on to say let your eyelids look right on! Proverbs 3:21 declares, *"My son, let not them depart from thine eyes..."* Let's not let God's Word depart from our eyes. Keep your eyes on the Word of God. That is the answer.

The believer is not to be moved by what he sees. Let me explain. II Corinthians 4:16-18 states, *"For which cause we faint not; but though our outward man perish, yet the inward man is renewed day by day. For our light affliction, which is but for a moment, worketh for us a far more exceeding weight of glory; while we look not at the things which are seen, but at the things which are not seen; for the things which are seen are temporal; but the things which are not seen are eternal."* Paul is implying that the believer doesn't need to look at the things which are seen, but the things which are not seen. You see many Christians have been programmed to believe that the things which can be seen are more real than the Creator of them. He goes on to write that the things which can be seen are temporal. The word temporal means subject to change. Everything that can be seen with the physical eye is temporary; it is subject to change. Colossians 3:2 says, "Set your affection on things above, not on things on the earth." Things above are not the stars in the sky, or the moon, or the sun. They are things of the spirit. Faith is actually seeing what can't be seen in the natural.

Let's take a look at Peter. Now we know the story in Matthew 14:22-31. So let me just explain. We must understand first of all that Jesus was the embodiment of the Word. John 1 declared that, "In the beginning was the word and the word was with God and the word was God....and the word became flesh and dwelt among us...." So as long as Peter's eyes were on the word, which was Jesus, when he stepped out of the boat and began to walk on water, he didn't sink. . But the moment he took his eyes off the word, he sank. As long as he was keeping his eyes on the word he was fine. Saints, that is why we must keep our eyes on the Word, then we can walk on water.

You don't talk about your financial problem, you ***speak*** *to your financial problem!*

An example of this would be simple. You know God's Word says that He would provide. You have given the tithe and offerings, the bills are stacking up and yet your checkbook is in the red. What do you do? You don't look at the checkbook, you look at the Word. And you hold on to the Word of God. You don't talk about your financial problem, you speak to your financial problem and see what the Word of God says about it and you stand in faith and you believe it.

As a believer, don't be governed by what you see in the natural, only by what you see in the spirit realm and in God's Word. II Corinthians 5:7 says, *"For we walk by faith and not by sight."* Faith causes you to see the things that have not been revealed to the senses. In other words, we are not to be governed by what we see and hear in the natural, we are not to walk by our physical senses. We are to walk by faith. Walk by the Word of God. God's Word, not circumstances, is to dictate to our spirits.

How can our light affliction work for us a far more exceeding and eternal weight of Glory? Only when we get our eyes off what we can see and get them on what we cannot see. We must focus our vision on things eternal. The old song says, "Turn your eyes upon Jesus, Look full into to His wonderful face, and the things of this earth will grow strangely dim, in the light of His glory and grace." So our light affliction will be for just a moment if we are looking at the right things.

In order to begin to look through the eye of faith, the physical eye must become focused on the Word. David said, *"Mine eyes are ever toward the Lord...."* And Jesus said in Matthew 6:22-23, *"The light of the body is the eye: if therefore thine eye be single, thy whole body shall be full of light. But if thy eye be evil, thy whole body shall be full of darkness. If therefore the light that is in thee be darkness, how great is that darkness!"* The Word of God will create a third eye, the eye of Faith. We begin to see what the Word of God says.

The Word of God lights the path in the unseen realm. It is the illuminating light that makes plain the view of the unseen. Psalm 119:105 declares, *"Thy word is a lamp unto my feet, and a light unto my path."* Psalm 119:130 says also, *"The entrance of thy words giveth light...."* When we see the Word of God, it lights the path of our life so we can walk by faith. The very entrance of the Word of God gives light to us to see the unseen. Keeping the Word of God before your eyes will create the image of that Word within you. You begin to see it. It becomes more real to you than even the things which you can see with your physical eye. Many people fail because they see themselves failing. They allow the Word of God to depart from their eyes. Quit looking at the wrong things and start seeing the God things. That is seeing through the eye of Faith.

SUCCESSFUL THINKING

A mind is a terrible thing to waste

The essence of who we are is in our thought life.

"Finally my brothers, whatever is true, whatever is noble, whatever is right, whatever is pure, whatever is lovely, whatever is admirable - if anything is excellent or praiseworthy - think about such things."
PHILIPPIANS 4:8 NIV

"Beloved, I pray that you may prosper in all things and be in health, just as your soul prospers."
III JOHN 2 (NKJV)

John was an old man when he wrote one of the last letters to be included in the canon of the scripture. He had walked with Jesus since he was a young man. John realized that the prosperity and success of our whole life, as well as the health of our bodies, hinged on the condition of our soul. It is what is in us that controls what comes out of us and ultimately all of our life experiences. When our soul succeeds, our life succeeds.

Our soul is our mind, will, and emotions. It is the dimension of man that deals with the mental realm. Our mind is our reasoning and thinking process. Our emotions are our feelings and our will, is the deciding and choosing processes. This plays a very vital role in our success in life.

Our thinking controls our life. Proverbs 23:7 says, *"For as a man THINKETH in his heart SO IS HE."* Our thoughts direct our decisions, actions, and feelings. Success is an attitude. Success is a way of thinking. Success is easily available to all who want it, believe they can have it, and put their desires into action.

Success has no secrets. Many who achieve it readily tell their story of devoting years to their efforts, to their dreams, and thoughts before they became successful. The main theme is always the same, in most every case. They "thought" about it before they achieved it. It was in their mind. They had successful thinking before they became successful.

Henry Ford said, "If you think you can, you're right. If you think you can't, you're right." You have to believe you can be successful before you will ever succeed. I know this sounds like a cliché, but take the time to stop and think about it. Where else can this extraordinary life begin? Your thinking creates your life experience; it's not the other way around. So no matter what you thought like before, you can change your thinking and change your life. We have been programmed to live within the limitations that other people have set for us. Think about this — the average person has over fifty thousand thoughts each and every day. In a sixteen-hour waking day, that works out to about one thought per second. Think of the activity going on within your mind. Every success, every revolution, every war, every invention, every song and every book has begun with thoughts. You and I have fifty thousand opportunities every day to create something that is wonderful and life changing.

> "Are you what you think you are?"
> If you think you are beaten, you are;
> If you thought you dare not, you don't;
> If you'd like to win but you think you can't,

It is almost certain you won't.
If you think you'll lose, you've lost,
for out in the world you'll find success begins
with a person's will - it's all in the state of mind.
If you think you're outclassed, you are;
you've got to think high to rise;
You've got to be sure of yourself before
you can ever win the prize.
Life's battles don't always go
To the stronger or faster man;
but the man who wins is
the man who thinks he can!

"I beseech ye therefore, brethren, by the mercies of God that you present your bodies a living sacrifice, holy and acceptable unto God which is your reasonable service. Be not conformed to this world, but be ye transformed by the renewing of your mind, that ye may prove what is that good, and acceptable, perfect will of God."
ROMANS 12:1, 2

The New Living Translation says, *"Don't copy the behavior and customs of this world, but let God transform you into a new person by changing the way you think. Then you will know what God wants you to do."* Whether we realize it or not, our greatest difficulties usually lie in the way we think about the situations and issues of life. The process that God uses to transform our life is the method of changing our thinking. When we change our thinking we get transformed into His image.

Transformed is to go through a complete change in form or kind. The Greek word is *metomorpho.* It means to go through a complete change in form such as the caterpillar does when it comes out of its cocoon as a butterfly.

So renewing the mind is both taking off old thoughts, and putting on the thoughts of God (Eph. 4:22-24). The habitual thoughts of our life control how we live. What you think determines what you believe; what you believe determines how you act; and how you act determines how you live.

Every lack or problem in your life started as a wrong thought. Every blessing or positive change in your life started with a right thought (Matthew 12:35).

Every individual has a job to do with their mind; that is to renew it on a daily basis. You see, our mind has two functions. One, it has an imagination; and two, it has a memory. Your imagination pre-plays what you want to have, or happen in your life. Your memory replays your past experiences, good or bad. So many people spend more time dwelling on their past than they ever do their present or future. They keep pressing the "play" button on their tape player of life, instead of hitting "record" and capturing a vision of what is ahead for them.

When your thinking changes, then your behavior and actions are changed, and when that happens you are transformed.

Our mind is the birthplace of our thinking. Therefore, we are required to change our thinking. If not, we will open the door to the present-day negative things of the world and we will be acting just like every other negative person we know.

When your thinking changes, then your behavior and actions are changed, and when that happens you are transformed. Your thoughts are the most powerful forces that shape your life. Your thoughts are like a train. So you must ask yourself this question: *Are my thoughts taking me where I want to go?*

How we combat the negative thought patterns that come into our minds is simple. We must first find out how they come. II Corinthians 2:11 reads, *"Lest Satan should get an advantage of us; we are not ignorant of his DEVICES."* And II Corinthians 10:3-5 says, *"For though we walk in the flesh, we do not war after the flesh; For the weapons of our warfare are not carnal but mighty through God to the pulling down of strongholds; casting down imaginations, and every high thing that exalts itself against the knowledge of God and bringing into captivity every THOUGHT to the obedience of*

Christ." The word "device" in II Corinthians 2:11 is the same word in the Greek for the word "thoughts" in II Corinthians 10:5. The Greek word is *noema* which means a perception, purpose or the intellect, disposition itself-devise, mind, or thought. So the negative devices that Satan uses against us are thoughts that he drops into our minds. That is why you and I are to renew our minds.

You will remember that the location where Jesus Christ was crucified in Jerusalem was called "Golgatha," which meant the "place of the skull." Jesus was completely effective in destroying the works of the devil when He was crucified on the cross at Calvary. Therefore, if we will be effective in this life, the first field of conflict where we must learn to excel and succeed against negative thoughts is the battleground of our minds. It's the place of the skull. Your battles, your failures, and your successes are first fought in your mind.

The first thing God did in creation was separate light from darkness. God's Word confronts wrong thinking in our lives, so we can recognize those thoughts and choose to change. We have to choose to change our thinking, because God will not come against our wills.

The enemy of our success will continually drop "thoughts" (devices) into our minds and they will always be negative and destined for failure. The way to combat these negative thoughts is with God's thoughts, which is God's Word.

You see, what happens when Satan places a thought in your mind, if you dwell on that thought you begin to take knowledge of that thought, and after you have taken knowledge, which is defined as "to know, perceive, be acquainted with," it then becomes an imagination. An imagination is a purpose of thought, an image in your mind, a word picture. If the negative thought becomes an imagination, then it will become a stronghold and then it controls you. A stronghold is anything in your life that is larger than your personal ability to deal with by your own will.

So take those thoughts and bring them into captivity to the obedience of Christ. This means that once you receive those thoughts, combat them with the positive power of God's thoughts. When this is accomplished, the negative thoughts will be reversed. You will go from weakness to strength, sickness to healing, blindness to vision, deafness to hearing, death to life, doubt to faith, from a loser to a winner, from fear to great faith, to an attitude of "can't do it" to "I can do all things through Christ which strengthens me."

If we want to live the kind of life God has in mind for us, we must trade our thoughts for His thoughts. We must lay down the thoughts of negativism and instead, pick up the wisdom of the Bible. God tells us in

"Seek ye the Lord while he may be found, call ye upon him while he is near; Let the wicked forsake his way, and the unrighteous man his thoughts; and let him return unto the Lord, he will have mercy upon him; and to our God, for he will abundantly pardon. For my thoughts are not your thoughts, neither are your ways my ways, saith the Lord. For as the heavens are higher than the earth, so are my ways higher than your ways, and my thoughts your thoughts. For as the rain cometh down, and the snow from heaven, and returneth not thither, but watereth the earth, and maketh it bring forth and bud, that it may give seed to the sower, and bread to the eater; so shall my word be that goeth forth out of my mouth: it shall not return unto me void, but it shall accomplish that which I please, and it shall prosper in the thing whereto I sent it."

ISAIAH 55:6-11

So remember successful thinking will bring forth successful results.

Prayer: Your Connection To Success

"Then he prayed, 'O LORD, God of my master Abraham, give me success today and show kindness to my master Abraham."
Genesis 24:12 (NIV)

In this chapter we will define what prayer is, what prayer does, how to pray, and hindrances to prayer. First, let's define what prayer is. Prayer is simply communication. It is dialogue, not monologue. God speaks to us and we speak to Him, or vice versa. Obviously the basis of any transaction in life is that of communication. That means we must open up our mouth and speak. Then we must open up our ears and listen. Two-way communication. That is awesome! We have a God that is not deaf. He desires to communicate with His people.

Think about the society that we live in today. Everything is based upon communication. The largest companies are telecommunications. Cellular phones, pagers, email, faxes, websites, etc. Why? All because they want to make communication easier and simpler for us in the 21st century. All financial, business, and relationship success in this day and age is based upon communication. To achieve spiritual success one must learn the art of communication — communication with God. Of course, He is the designer of success. So prayer must be the fuel to achieve success in life. Regardless of anyone's ability, he or she will fail if the pursuit of success is not backed by prayer.

Notice the scripture in Genesis 24:12. The person prayed to God to give him SUCCESS. If you read on, you will find that is exactly what he received. When you pray specific prayers you will get specific results. Pastor J. Hugh Rose of Harrison Hills Church in Jewett, Ohio, who was my pastor growing up always used to say, "Don't stop praying and don't stop believing in the results of your prayers." God does answer prayer. I have never forgotten this powerful truth.

There is an old song that says, "Saints, don't stop praying for the Lord is nigh, Saints, don't stop praying He'll hear your cry, for Lord has promised, His Word is true, Saints, don't stop praying He'll answer you". Prayer is the key to all success. But it must be faith-filled prayer — prayer that believes what's being prayed.

Prayer plays a great role in my life. I believe I am where I am because of prayer. Maybe not necessarily my prayers, but simply prayer. Prayer from family, prayer from friends, simply people praying for me. The result is that prayer brings divine health, prayer brings prosperity and provision, prayer brings abundance, prayer brings peace of mind, and prayer brings success.

The most powerful thing a person can do is pray. Communicating with God through prayer is the life source of a person's success. Prayer is the basic building block of all spiritual enterprise. You see when we pray, it enables God to do what he can. Prayer can do anything God can do. John Wesley said, "God does nothing but in answer to prayer." If you don't like where you are in life, try prayer. Talk to the creator, let him talk to you. You find peace and contentment in a relationship with God.

Prayer must become a habit. In Luke 14:16, Jesus made it a habit to go daily to the Synagogue. The secret to your success is hidden in your daily routine. Make prayer the first thing you do in the morning and the last thing you do before you fall asleep. The Apostle Paul, told us to "Pray without ceasing". What he meant was pray all the time. Always be communicating with God. You will never achieve your success in life until your prayer life becomes habitual. You might attain a certain amount of money, you might obtain a new car, a bigger house, etc., but you will never achieve true success without a relationship with God through prayer. People never decide their future. They decide their habits, and their habits decide their future. Make prayer a daily habit and then see what your future will be. Now here are some strategies for a successful prayer life.

> *People never decide their future. They decide their habits, and their habits decide their future.*

Find a designated place to pray, a place that is far from distractions and interruptions. In Matthew 14:23, Jesus sent the multitudes away and went up in the evening into a mountain to pray. Luke 5:16 states that He withdrew himself in the wilderness and prayed. Find a private place to pray where you will not be distracted or interrupted. We live in a time today where everyone is so busy. Everything is fast paced and moving so quickly. We don't even know how to relax. Most vacations today are "working" vacations where one has to take his or her career work with them. This kind of mindset today has taken effect on one's prayer life. We give the excuse, we simply don't have the time. So turn off the television, take the phone off the hook, turn your mobile phone off, shut the door, turn off your pager and be alone with God. Distractions can destroy the communication lines with God. I have a private place in our home where I love to go to and be alone with God. It is a place of solitude. It is private and it is where I can talk to God and He to me.

Find a public place to pray. Yes, a public place. Well, what about the ACLU and all the liberal media that says keep prayer out of the public place. Well, that is their opinion and it is not constitutional, it is scriptural to pray in public. In Acts 16:13, Paul on the sabbath went out of the city to the riverside and prayed. When I used to live in South Bend, Indiana, during my lunch break from work, I would go to the St. Joe River and sit on the bank underneath the trees and just pray. Those were some of the most intimate times I had with the Lord. It was in public, but for me, it was also private. In Acts 21:5, Paul and the disciples went out of the city and kneeled down on the shore and prayed. When we vacation every year we usually go to Mexico, Florida or the Carolina's. To be there near the ocean is always memorable to my spiritual life. I will wake early in the morning and go to the beach and just walk and pray and watch the sun come up. It is amazing the peace and solitude you find when you look at God's creation. It seems to make your dilemmas or problems seem so small. It lets you see and acknowledge the greatness of God in your life, because if He can cause the sun to come up in the morning, he can take care of anything in your life.

Find a church to pray in. In Acts 22:17, Paul went to the temple to pray. In Acts 3, Peter and John were going daily to the temple to pray. Going to church to pray was a part of the early church's daily habits. Most all churches are open during the day for anyone to come into and find either a sanctuary or a prayer room. Before you go to work, on your lunch hour, or on your way home, find a church you can take a few moments to pray in. You will find the atmosphere conducive to being close to God. If you are a member of a local church, when there is a prayer meeting called by the leadership, do everything you can to be a part of it. Make prayer a priority in your life, not just a quick fix to a problem you are facing, because prayer is about a long-term relationship between you and God.

A remarkable illustration of prayer is found in a story told by John Wesley. He was once riding through a dark wood, carrying with him a large sum of money entrusted to his safe keeping. All at once a sense of fear came over him, and dismounting from his horse, he offered up a prayer of protection. Years afterward Wesley was called to see a dying man. This man told the preacher that at the time Wesley had passed through the wood many years before, the man had been lying in wait to rob him. He told Wesley that he had noticed him dismounting and resuming his journey. What appeared to be an armed attendant riding beside him so filled him with awe and great fear that he abandoned his purpose.

Prayer is really our hearts' desire for oneness with our Divine Creator. It is our link to the supernatural. We do the natural and God does the supernatural. It is literally what Phillips Brooks described it to be, the gate between God and the soul.

Author and Pastor George Brantley said, "The time to learn how to pray is now, not when a crisis arises." Eighty-six percent of Americans profess belief in a prayer-answering God, but only 58% of them set aside time to pray each day. Prayer doesn't just happen, you must make time to pray. The Jews in Acts 3:1 and Acts 10:9, had three scheduled hours of daily prayer, 9am, 12 noon, and 3pm. I am not saying that you have to do it like they did, but you can schedule time in your day that you will spend with God. It could be early in the morning before the sun comes up and before you go to work. In Mark 1:35, Jesus would get up before dawn and pray. The issue is you must make prayer the priority. To those of you who are "late-nighters", pray late at night. In Luke 6:12, Jesus went into the mountain and prayed all night long. So when is the right time to pray? Simply when you pray. Acts 1:14 stated that they continued in prayer. Paul said pray always and without ceasing. So you can constantly be in communication with God. The "where's" and the "specifics" help you with the atmosphere. The "when" is the necessity for spiritual advancement and success. So make the "when" an "always."

HINDRANCES TO AN EFFECTIVE PRAYER LIFE

Unanswered prayer is not the result of God's unwillingness to use his power, but because of hindrances we allow to overcome us. You see, God's desire is to answer our prayers. He gave us His Word to pray according to His will.

"Jesus answered and said unto them, Verily I say unto you, If ye have faith, and doubt not, ye shall not only do this which is done to the fig tree, but also if ye shall say unto this mountain, Be thou removed, and be thou cast into the sea; it shall be done. And all things, whatsoever ye shall ask in prayer, believing, ye shall receive."
MATTHEW 21:21-22

Prayer that brings results must be based upon God's Word. When you have a problem that you are praying about, start with the answer. All answers to life are found in the Bible. John 15:7 says,

"If you abide in me and my words abide in you, you shall ask what ye will, and it shall be done unto you."

Even though we can have results in our prayers, we can also have hindrances. We must eradicate hindering elements from our prayers if we want results. When any or all of these known hindrances are removed, we are ready to persist and persevere in prayer until our answer comes.

The first hindrance is an improper husband-and-wife relationship. This can be found in I Peter 3:7. When there is contention, strife and disharmony in a home this will affect the prayers of that couple. It is so vitally important to a husband and wife to have a right relationship, if not, they cannot pray effectively. Never go to sleep angry with each other. Resolve the conflict before you go to sleep. Learn to communicate with one another and talk things out. Don't let anyone or anything come between you and your spouse. The relationship between a husband and wife is likened unto Christ and His Church.

The second hindrance is sin in our life. David said in Psalm 66:18, *"If I regard iniquity in my heart, the Lord will not hear me."* Isaiah 59:1-2 states, *"Behold the Lord's hand is not shortened, that it cannot save; neither his ear heavy, that it cannot hear; But your iniquities have separated you and your God, and your sins have hid his face from you, that he will not hear you."* Actively engaging in sinful practices, never repenting, or even being hypocritical will stop the answer to your prayers. *The cure?* Repentance of your sins. You must have faith and ask God to forgive you and believe that he does. Paul said, "I die daily." What did he mean? He meant *repentance.* Repentance must be a daily activity. No one is perfect.

The third hindrance is not asking according to God's will. I John 5:14-15 in the Amplified Bible says, *"And this is the confidence (the assurance, the priviledge of boldness) which we have in Him: (we are sure) that if we ask anything (make any request) according to His will (in agreement with His own plan), He listens to and hears us. And if (since) we (positively) know that He listens to us in whatever we ask, we also know (with settled and absolute knowledge) that we have (granted us as our present possessions) the requests made of Him."* God's will in this context is God's Word. Neither are we to ask God for things contrary to His will for our personal lives. His Word and His plan for your life should be considered when you pray. Find the answer in the Bible and pray that scripture. There are many things you and I don't have in life because we don't realize in God's Word that they are available to us. Tradition and religion limits us to receive from God. If it is in the Word of God it is available to you today.

The fourth hindrance is doubt and unbelief. Unbelief is when a person believes there is a God, but doesn't believe His Word. Doubt is one of the biggest hindrances we have to fight in our prayer life. Doubt and unbelief are when you know what God says and you second-guess it. Jesus said in Mark 9:23, *"...if thou canst believe, all things are possible to him that believeth."* Doubt and unbelief do not disqualify you. Your struggle is proof of your need for faith. You see doubt and unbelief causes your faith to be short-charged. Mark 11:23 stated that we should not doubt in our hearts. If we don't we will receive whatsoever we saith. Stay away from negative influences and people who will try to plant seeds of doubt and unbelief in your life. I have decided to separate myself from these kinds of people. I don't give criticism the time of day. Most critics and criticism come as a form to destroy not to build up. These influences will be a hindrance to your prayer life and ultimately your success.

There are many more hindrances that can be named (that's another book). So take these four hindrances and eradicate them out of your life and see your prayers answered.

When you learn to pray, you will understand that prayer will not only change circumstances but it will change you! If you desire to be a success in life, PRAY! Ask God to give you success. He said, *"...ask and you shall receive..."* (Matthew 7:7)

TITHING: YOUR KEY FOR SUCCEEDING

"Money talks, but it doesn't say when it is coming back...."

That, my friend, might be true from a carnal perspective. But it is not to be perceived that way in the Kingdom of God. God has a plan for prosperity and that plan has a beginning. TITHING. Tithing is not the idea of some preacher so he doesn't have to work a secular job. Tithing is God's idea.

"Honor the Lord with thy substance, and with the firstfruits of all thine increase: So shall thy barns be filled with plenty, and thy presses shall aburst out with new wine."
PROVERBS 3:9-10

Some people don't tithe because they are not taught. Then others do not tithe because of a misunderstanding of the place of God's law in the Bible. They will say that, "tithing is in the Old Testament and we are not under the law but under grace." Tithing is not a mosaic innovation, but it is a legalization of what Abraham had done voluntarily 400 years before the law came. Tithing is not a carryover from the law, it is a carryover from Abraham (Heb. 7:1-9).

Tithing is a principle. There is a difference between principles and commandments. A commandment is something you obey as long as it is in effect. A principle is something that you live by on a constant basis. The duration of a commandment is subject to change, but a principle is unchangeable.

Let me ask you a question. What are you giving to God? God gave His best to us. He gave His only begotten son.

"For God so loved the world that he gave
his only begotten son, that whosoever believeth in him
should not perish but have everlasting life."
JOHN 3:16

King David refused to offer to God the things that cost him nothing. David bought the threshing floor and the oxen for fifty pieces of silver and then offered them unto the Lord as an offering. We live in a society that wants a handout. We expect everything to come to us for free. The only thing that is free in this life is one thing — salvation. Jesus Christ paid the price for that on the cross of Calvary when He gave His life to die for the sin of mankind. Beside that, there is a price to pay for something. Prosperity has its price and that price begins with the spiritual principle of tithing.

Folks, God wants your first and He wants your best!

1. EXODUS 23:19 - *"The first of the first fruits of thy land and thou shalt bring into the house of the Lord thy God...."*

2. LEVITICUS 23:10 - *"Speak unto the children of Israel, and say unto them, when ye be come into the land which I shall give unto you, and shall reap the harvest thereof, then ye shall bring a sheaf of the firstfruits of your harvest unto the priest...."*

3. NUMBERS 18:12 - *"All the best of the oil, and all the best of the wine, and of the wheat, the firstfruits of them which they shall offer unto the Lord, them have I given thee."*

4. PROVERBS 3:9-10 - *"Honour the Lord with thy substance, and with thy first fruits of all thine increase: So shall thy barns be filled with plenty, and thy presses shall burst out with new wine."*

You see the Lord considers your tithe HIS. Leviticus 27:30 states, *"And all the tithe of the land, whether of the seed of the land, or of the fruit of the tree, is the Lord's: it is holy unto the Lord."*

WHAT IS THE TITHE?

The tithe is "one tenth" or 10% of your increase. It means to give 1/10 of your income to God. You see, tithing is like have an insurance policy with God as the backer. You can't get any insurance policy like that from any agency in the world. Tithing is your opportunity to declare your independence from the world's system. The kingdom of God is never in a recession. Why? Because God owns everything. Psalm 24:1 says that the *"earth is the Lord's and the fulness thereof...."* He says that the silver is His and the gold is His. He owns the cattle on a thousand hills. When you tithe, you make your profession that you are subject to God's economy and not the world's economy. You need to declare with your mouth that depression, inflation, poverty, lack, and debt have no power over you!

"You shall truly tithe all the increase of your grain that the field produces year by year."
DEUTERONOMY 14:22

No promise of God is manifested unless we are obedient to God's Word. Let us, therefore, be obedient to God in the area of tithing. This must be acted upon. Our lack is caused by our disobedience to the Word. Not tithing is robbing God. And when you rob God, you rob yourself of His blessings. My friend, God is not going to enforce tithing on you. But the person who is "in Christ" understands that "His commandments are not burdensome" (I John 5:3). Tithing paves the way for blessings. When a person does not tithe, they break the law! Not man's legal law, not the Law of Moses, but God's beneolent law. It will not work for them. God only rewards obedience.

WHY SHOULD I TITHE?

First of all we must understand the tithe belongs to the Lord. Leviticus 27:30 states, *"And all the tithe of the land, whether of the seed of the land or of the fruit of the tree, is the Lord's. It is holy to the Lord."* The first 10% belongs to God. The remaining 90% of your income is really the 100% you have to work with. All your giving and sowing comes from your 90%.

The second reason is that the tithe is holy to God. *Why?* Because God calls it holy. It is the power of the dime, the power of the tenth. Whether or not it is holy to you depends on your heart's attitude and your submission to Jesus Christ and His Word.

The third reason is found in Malachi 3:10. *"Bring all the tithe into the storehouse, that there may be food in my house...."* That food enables the Word of God to be brought forth and taught in his house. Therefore, the tithe you give back to God provides food (information, resources) for God's work.

The fourth reason is that you may fear the Lord thy God always (Deuteronomy 14:22-23). The question may be asked, "Where do I tithe?" You tithe into the storehouse (Malachi 3:10, Dueteronomy 26:2). The House of God. Your local Church. The Church that you belong to on a consistent basis. The place where you get fed by the Word of God.

BENEFITS OF TITHING

"Will a man rob God? Yet you have robbed me! But you say, In what way have we robbed you? In tithes and offerings. You are cursed with a curse, for you have robbed me, even this whole nation. Bring all the tithe into the storehouse, that there may be food in my house, and try me now in this, says the Lord of hosts, if I will not open for you the windows of heaven and pour out for you such a blessing that there will not be room enough to receive it. And I will rebuke the devourer for your sakes, so that he will not destroy the fruit of your ground, nor shall the vine

bear fruit for you in the field, says the Lord of hosts; And all the nations
will call you blessed, for you will be a delightful land,
says the Lord of hosts."
MALACHI 3:8-17

Here is a list of the benefits of tithing:

1. You free yourself from the list of those who rob God.
2. You free yourself from the curse and become blessed.
3. You will enjoy the Word of God being taught.
4. The Lord will prove Himself to you.
5. The windows of heaven will open to you revealed knowledge.
6. The Lord will pour out a blessing.
7. The blessing will be larger than you can contain.
8. God will rebuke the devourer (Satanic opposition) for you.
9. The fruit of your ground will not be destroyed.
10. You will be fruitful and have increase.
11. All people will call you blessed.
12. You will be a delightsome (happy) household.
13. The Lord will spare you.
14. The Lord will give you power to create wealth. (Deut. 8:18)
15. The Lord will delight in your prosperity. (Psalm 35:27)
16. You will eat the best of the land. (Isaiah 1:19)
17. Your house will be filled with plenty. (Proverbs 3:9-10)
18. Your cupboards and closets will be filled.
19. You will be given the opportunity to declare your independence from the world's economic system. (Duet.26:3-5)
20. You will be known by the Lord.

God will cause every blessing that has your name written on it to be directed to you and opposition cannot stop it. Folks, He said there will not be "room enough." That means a large enough quantity, plenty, and measureless. Just think about it. When you obey God's Word and the principles that are in it, your income can be measureless. Just think, so much money coming in that you cannot even count it. The billionaire, John Getty, said if you can count your money you don't have a million dollars. The possibilities are measureless. My friend, your road to financial success begins with tithing. It is mathematically the tenth. It is scriptural because it is our responsibility. It is a moral debt we owe to God. It is also economical because it is an investment with a return of 100%. It now becomes spiritual because it causes blessing. Tithing is a "have to" and it is a "get to." You don't have to be blessed, you get to be blessed. You don't *have* to be successful, you *get* to be successful.

FINANCIAL PROSPERITY: A BYPRODUCT OF SUCCESS

"Beloved, I wish above all things that thou mayest prosper, even as thy soul prospereth."
III JOHN 2

We go to schools to become equipped to earn it. Then we spend almost the rest of our lives, 40-60 hours a week, actually earning it. We invest countless hours in thought and discussion on how we're going to handle it. We walk around shopping malls determining how we're going to spend it. We get caught up more often than we would care to admit worrying that we won't have enough of it. We dream and scheme to figure out ways to acquire more of it. Arguments over it are among the leading causes of marital disintegration, business partner breakups, and governmental shutdowns. Despair over losing it causes suicides. The obsession with getting it causes many of society's crimes. The absence of it causes many of society's nightmares.

Some call it the root of all evil. Some call it the means for great good. But we cannot afford to ignore the reality or the importance of MONEY.

There is a story of a man who jumped off the Brooklyn Bridge and drowned. He had just had the worst day of his life, just lost $100,000.00 in the stock market. Then there was another man, it was the greatest day of his life. He had just won $100,000.00 in the lottery, so he had gotten drunk and in his celebration fell off the Brooklyn Bridge and died. Such a tragedy, all over money.

The Bible doesn't ignore it. In fact, it speaks to the subject head on, with eyes open and no holds barred. The Bible claims to be the single best guidebook on money management matters ever written. Some 2000 passages in the Bible refer to the use of money. Two-thirds of Jesus' parables make some reference to it. Let's look at the wisdom of God's Word on this subject.

You might not necessarily want to be mega rich. You would just like to be released from the chains of debt, along with worry and frustration over finances. This is what God wants for you.

What I want to deal with in this chapter is you as an individual riding on the road of financial success. What avenues to take and cash flow strategies for your financial freedom. Money! For many people, it's the greatest cause of stress in their lives. Being married for twelve years, which is not long considering some of the precious folks who have been together for 20, 30, or even 50 years, (for which I honor you!), I can tell you that the majority of our disagreements came from conversations concerning our family finances. Most people sacrifice things much more valuable than money in order to get more of it. They spend valuable time that could have been shared with their children, their families, and their friends. Some even destroy their health to work harder and make more money.

Nothing teaches character better than generosity."
-JIM ROHN

The key today is not to work harder, but to work smarter. As you will see, I am going to give you Biblical examples and personal examples concerning God's plan for becoming financially independent. As I shared in the previous chapters concerning wealth and prosperity, I want to focus this chapter on the means of financial prosperity and accumulating wealth to become financially independent.

Our country was founded by visionaries who believed in free enterprise through individual determination, and the backbone of God's will and purpose. His will for people is to be financially independent. Even in the Bible the great men that God used were wealthy and prosperous and a majority of them were entrepreneurs. What is so sad today is that many non-believers in today's society are using God's principles for financial success and they are becoming financially blessed. God's principles will work for whoever applies them. The problem with many believers today is that they are just lazy. Sitting around waiting for the blessings to show up. Attempting to live from one financial miracle to another. Please don't get me wrong, I believe in financial miracles. There were plenty in the Bible and plenty that have happened to me. We must learn to live as financial managers. We must remember that God is the one who gives us the POWER to CREATE wealth. The power is the ability. God has given everyone an ability to create wealth on this earth.

Wealth is a neutral term. The dictionary defines "wealth" as "a large aggregate of real and personal property; an abundance of those material or worldly things that men desire to possess." It also states, "all material objects which have economic utility: all property possessing monetary value." You and I both know that it can be used in a positive way or a negative way. God's purpose for prosperity is that we might become a channel of His blessing to others (Ephesians 4:8, I Timothy 6:18, 17-19, II Corinthians 8:1-15, II Corinthians 9:8-9). This must be our true motivation for accumulating wealth.

PROSPERITY: GOD'S DESIRE FOR US

God wants you to be prosperous. The Bible, which is God's Word, boldly declares, from the book of Genesis to the book of Revelation that it's God's will that you walk in prosperity in every area of your life.

In Genesis, God boldly declared to Abram that He would bless him and make a blessing. Further, God told Abram that He would make his name great (Genesis 12:2). When God told Abram that he would bless him to be a blessing, God was saying to Abram that He was going to abundantly prosper him with prosperity so that he could be in a position to bless others. How can you be in a position to be a blessing to others if you aren't blessed yourself? You can't! The word "bless" used in Genesis 12:2 is from the Hebrew word *barak* which means abundantly; and, the word "blessing" is from the word *berakah* which comes from "barak" and means prosperity. My friend, God was saying to Abram that He was going to abundantly prosper him in every area of his life, including finances. Genesis 13:2 and 6 confirms that God prospered Abram financially.

"And Abram was VERY RICH in cattle, in silver, and in gold. And the land was not able to bear them (Abram & Lot), that they might dwell together: for their SUBSTANCE was GREAT, so that they could not dwell together."
GENESIS 13:2

Take note, Abram was VERY RICH. The definition of "very", according to the *Random House Dictionary,* means "in a high degree." He was rich in a high degree. Think about this, the father of our faith was a very rich man. Are you so prosperous and rich in substance that you and your family have to separate because the land cannot contain you and the substance possessed by you combined? God so prospered Abraham that he and Lot could not even dwell together in the same region because of the magnitude of their substance. They were abundantly prosperous! They were very rich!

> *Only by giving are you able to receive more than you already have.*

Now Galatians 3:29 declares that *"if ye be in Christ, then are ye Abraham's seed, and heirs according to the promise."* Therefore, God's covenant with Abraham to abundantly prosper him is also God's covenant with us. Jesus is the mediator of a better covenant, which was established upon better promises (Hebrews 8:6). Therefore, God's covenant of prosperity is also included in our new covenant which has been appropriated through being born again.

So God not only desires that His people prosper, but He promises that they will prosper. Psalm 1:3 says, *"And he shall be like a tree planted by the rivers of water, that bringeth forth his fruit in his season; his leaf also shall not wither; and whatsoever he doeth shall prosper."* Psalm 122:6-7, *"Pray for the peace of Jerusalem: they shall prosper that love thee. Peace be within thy walls, and prosperity within thy palaces."*

FINANCIAL PROSPERITY IS THE WILL OF GOD

"The blessing of the Lord, it maketh RICH,
and he addeth no sorrow to it."
PROVERBS 10:22

Financial prosperity is the will of God for every believer. Psalm 35:27 states, *"Let the Lord be magnified, which hath pleasure in the prosperity of his servant."* Without a doubt you have a right to prosper financially. The will of God should never be confusing. God is not the author of confusion. The will of God is simply the expression of the Word of God. Therefore, we must hear and do the Word of God and in that we will be doing the Will of God. The word "prosper or prosperity" is found over 90 times in the Bible. So beloved, God's will for us is prosperity.

DEFINITIONS OF PROSPERITY

Take note of the following definitions from the *New Lexicon Webster's Encyclopedic Dictionary of the English Language.*

- ***prosper*** - to thrive, to achieve financial success
- ***prosperity*** - the condition of being prosperous, the condition of high economic activity
- ***prosperous*** - financially successful

The Random House Dictionary definitions are as follows:

- ***prosper*** - to be successful, especially financially
- ***prosperity*** - the state or condition of being successful, especially financially
- ***prosperous*** - having or characterized by financial success

The Greek word translated "prosper" in III John 2 is the word, *euodoo*, which is from two words, "good" and "journey." It is a good journey. The Strong's Exhaustive Concordance of the Bible adds, "to succeed in business affairs." Simply put, in our journey through life, God desires for us to succeed in our business affairs, which in turn results in a condition of high economic activity and financial prosperity and success.

THE PREREQUISITE TO PROSPERITY

As we shared in the previous chapter, tithing is a prerequisite to financial prosperity. In this next section, I want to talk about GIVING or SOWING.

> *"6 But this I say, He which soweth sparingly shall reap also sparingly; and he which soweth bountifully shall reap also bountifully. 7 Every man according as he purposeth in his heart, so let him give; not grudgingly, or of necessity: for God loveth a cheerful giver. 8 And God is able to make all grace abound toward you; that ye, always having all sufficiency in all things, may abound to every good work: 9 (As it is written, He hath dispersed abroad; he hath given to the poor: his righteousness remaineth for ever. 10 Now he that ministereth seed to the sower both minister bread for your food, and multiply your seed sown, and increase the fruits of your righteousness;) 11 Being enriched in every thing to all bountifulness, which causeth through us thanksgiving to God."*
>
> \- II CORINTHIANS 9:6-11

Our giving causes a supernatural connection that allows God to work in our finances. When a person gives, he or she is involving God in their finances. The results of giving are incredible and overwhelming. When something leaves your hand, then something leaves God's hand. Galatians 6:9 says, *"Be not deceived God is not mocked, whatsoever a man soweth that he shall also reap."*

Giving is a spiritual law. Think about this. It goes all the way back to Genesis, "As long as the earth remains there will be seedtime and harvest." There it is, the law of sowing and reaping. You sow a seed and you reap a harvest. It is pretty simple. The kind of seed you sow determines the kind of harvest you receive. It is law. You plant an apple seed, you get an apple tree. You plant a financial seed, you receive a financial harvest. It works my friend.

II Corinthians 9:6-11 is not talking about tithing. Here is the reason why. Verse nine says, "He hath dispersed abroad." The tithe is not dispersed abroad, the tithe is brought into the storehouse, or the local church. It continues to say, *"he hath given to the poor...."* The tithe does not go to the poor; it goes directly into the storehouse. Now verse six says that we can give sparingly or bountifully. The tithe is simply ten percent. So this passage of scripture is speaking about offerings.

Offerings are a very important part of our success in life. Our giving allows God to give to us. It is the law of sowing and reaping. This goes all the way back to Genesis 8:22, *"As long as the earth remains seedtime and harvest."* It is another spiritual law that brings success in our life.

"Give and it shall be given unto you; good measure, pressed down, shaken together, and running over, shall men give into your bosom. For with the same measure that ye mete withal it shall be measured to you again."
- LUKE 6:38

Notice that Jesus just didn't only say, "Give;" but he also said, "and it will be given unto you." Giving and receiving go together. It is only when we give that we get into a position to receive. What leaves your hand leaves God's hand.

> *"Giving is better than receiving because giving starts the receiving process."*
> - JIM ROHN

This is the law of divine reciprocity. You give and God gives in return. When you plant a seed, the ground yields a harvest. You see the ground can only give to you what you give to it.

Everything about God is about giving. He said in John 3:16, *"For God so loved the world that He GAVE..."* The very nature of God is giving. He gave His son and He reaped a harvest of millions of sons and daughters called the body of Christ, the church.

We live in a nation that has proved this over and over again. That is why America is so blessed with success. What other nation do you know that will go to war against a country and then when that country is defeated by America, we will take billions of dollars and rebuild that country. America is the most giving nation in the world. With the recent terrorist attacks on September 11, 2001, our nation once again proved its true motives and heart. America gave. Not only did it give in blood and labor, but, it gave of its finances. When it is all said and done, billions will have been given in personal and corporate finances. And because of that, America will be blessed. America gives and America will receive.

SUCCESSFUL GIVING

One may ask how we are to give. II Corinthians 9:7 says, *"Every man as he purposeth in his heart, so let him give, NOT GRUDGINGLY, or of NECESSITY; for God loveth a CHEERFUL GIVER."* As far as God is concerned, it is not how much is given, but "how it is given." Man may look on the outward appearance, but God looks on the heart. Man might see how much is given, but God sees how something is given.

Jesus took notice of how people gave. Mark 12:41 says, *"And Jesus sat over against the treasury, and beheld HOW the people cast money into the treasury..."* If Jesus was concerned then, he is concerned now. Make sure you are a cheerful giver. A cheerful giver is one who gives in faith. Because he or she knows that the amount that was given is nothing compared to what will be received and that has to make a person happy.

Let me share an example of how giving works.

In August of 1999, my wife and I were at Faith Week conference in Chicago, Illinois, at Pastor Robb and Linda Thompson's. While we were in the church service we felt impressed to give a certain amount in the offering for Jesse Duplantis, a $250 seed to be exact. Now, $250 might not be a lot of money to you, but we only had $265 in our checking account. So we were being stretched. Our faith was about to go on trial. A spirit of joy came over us as we both felt that was the right amount that God told us to write. On the memo of the check we wrote "DEBT FREE." You see we were identifying our seed so that we could receive a specific harvest. We were sowing so we could be "Debt Free." We had owed $25,000 on credit cards, vehicles, medical bills, etc. The next year, we had received a harvest of $7,000 in February, $2,000 in April and $16,000 by June, giving us a total of $25,000! You see my friend, giving works. God will honor His Word, your faith, your obedience, and His spiritual law. There is success in giving. There are two old songs, one that says, *"You can't beat God giving no matter how hard you try, the more you give, the more He'll give to you, so keep on giving because it's really true...."* The other declares, *"There's a joy in giving and I found it to be true, the more you give to Jesus, the more he's gonna give to you. So give till you just can't give anymore, even more than you can afford, you'll find your cup will overflow because you can't out give the Lord...."* That, my friend, is so true. Give and be successful! It really is true, it is more blessed to give than to receive.

The amount you give isn't important. What matters is what that amount represents in terms of your life.

Success Points For Life

"A Book is a friend; a good book is a good friend. It will talk when you want it to talk, and it will keep still when you want it to keep still - and there aren't many friends who know enough to do that."

– **Lymon Abbott**

"Success is not to be pursued; it is to be attracted by the person you become."

– **Jim Rohn**

"Success is not so much what we have as it is what we are."

– **Jim Rohn**

"Don't say, 'If I could, I would.' Say, 'If I can, I will.'"

– **Jim Rohn**

"Success is understanding that time is your most valuable possession."

"Success is having the resilience to rise again from defeat."

"Success is understanding that every mistake has its own penalty."

"If the Dream is big enough, the facts don't count."

– **Dexter Yeager**

"When you change your focus, you will change your results."

"What you give becomes an investment that will return to you multiplied at some point in the future."

Success Points For Life

"Don't let the things that matter most be at the mercy of the things that matter least."

– Dexter Yeager

"When you want something you have never had, you have to do something you have never done."

– Dr. Mike Murdock

"Character is the real foundation of all worthwhile success."

– John Hays Hammond

"It is not what he has, or even what he does which expresses the worth of a man, but what he is."

– Henri Frederic Amiel

"Think about your work as an expression of your love. Do what you love and the money will follow."

– Marsha Sinetar

"Obstacles are things a person sees when he takes his eyes off his goal."

– E. Joseph Cossman

"Failure is only the opportunity to begin again intelligently."

– Henry Ford

"A stumble may prevent a fall."

– English Proverb

"Success is more attitude than aptitude."

– Anonymous

"The highest reward for a person's toil is not what they get for it, but what they become by it."

– John Ruskin

Success Points For Life

"Don't confuse being rich with living a rich life. Being financially rich is a worthy goal, but living a rich life should be our primary mission."

– **Michael Angier**

"Achievement: Success is to be measured not so much by the position that one has reached in life as by the obstacles which he has overcome while trying to succeed."

– **Booker T. Washington**

"Success is to love God with all your heart, your mind, your soul, and your strength. To allow him to unlock the potential in your life and never settle for second best."

– **John Maxwell**

"Success is the power with which to acquire whatever one demands without violating the rights of others."

– **Andrew Carnegie**

"The whole secret of a successful life is to find out what one's destiny is and then do it."

– **Henry Ford**

"Dream big dreams; only big dreams have the power to move men's souls."

– **Marcus Aurelius**

"We are judged by what we finish, not by what we start."

– **Anonymous**

"A person with a clear purpose will make progress on even the roughest road. A person with no purpose will make no progress on even the smoothest road."

– **Thomas Carlyle**

SUCCESS POINTS FOR LIFE

"There is no limit to the inexhaustible power of God, and an "atom of faith" can blast a whole range of material mountains."

- HOWARD CARTER

"The greatest power that God has given to any individual is the power of prayer."

- KATHRYN KUHLMAN

"Faith is an eye that can see the invisible. Faith is an ear that hears what others do not hear. Faith is a hand that can touch the intangible."

- LESTER SUMRALL

"When the Power of God and faith are operative in your life, you are like a tank; you have the ability to move your position forward without taking any losses."

- RICK RENNER

"Great Victories come out of Great Battles."

- SMITH WIGGLESWORTH

"Insecurities caused by false principles in your belief window produce fear - and fear paralyzes success."

"Education is a progressive discovery of our own ignorance."

– WILL DURANT

"The Most important Goals we can establish are those that will last an eternity."

SUCCESS POINTS FOR LIFE

"The Bottom Line: If we have stopped learning, we have basically stopped living."

"The dictionary is the only place where success comes before work."

– **MARK TWAIN**

"That some achieve great success is proof to all that others can achieve it as well."

– **ABRAHAM LINCOLN**

"Flaming enthusiasm, backed by horse sense and persistence, is the quality that most frequently makes for success."

– **DALE CARNEGIE**

"Every really new idea looks crazy at first."

– **ALFRED NORTH WHITEHEAD**

"If there is any one secret of success, it lies in the ability to get the other person's point of view and see things from that person's angle as well as from your own."

–**HENRY FORD**

"Minds are like parachutes. They only function when they are open."

– **SIR JAMES DEWAR**

"Before speaking, consider the interpretation of your words as well as their intent."

– **ANDREW ALDEN**

"You either multiply your problems or multiply your luxuries."

Success Points For Life

"When you start doing what you really love to do, you'll never work another day in your life."

- Brian Tracy

"Continuous learning is the minimum requirement for success in any field."

- Dennis Waitley

"You can get everything you want in life if you just help enough other people get what they want."

- Zig Ziglar

"Imagination is more important than facts"

- Albert Einstein

"You will be the same person in five years except for the people you meet and the books you read."

- Charlie Jones

"The morality of the Bible is, after all, the safety of society."

- Francis Cassette Monfort

"Spend time putting together the best plan possible, then do it, drive it, move it, and make it happen."

– Karyn Conway

"Champions are not just born champions, they become Champions."

"In a moment of decision, the best thing you can do is the right thing to do. The worst thing you can do is nothing."

– Theodore Roosevelt

Success Notes For My Life

About the Author

Robert Yanok is Senior Pastor of CitiChurch in Mansfield, Ohio. CitiChurch is a dynamic and vibrant congregation of people who desire to change their generation to come under the Lordship of Jesus Christ. It is one of the fastest growing churches in North Central Ohio. He is also President and CEO of Robert Yanok International, a seminar and resource company geared to motivating and developing people for an extraordinary lifestyle.

Rob's messages are designed to empower God's people to rise above and move beyond their most difficult changes and challenges in life. His message of principle, purpose and power bring about immediate and long-term results. Avoiding quick fixes and plastic answers, he provides his audience with simple but profound strategies for living an extraordinary life.

Speaking with the dynamics and sensitivity developed by his strength as a pastor, teacher, and counselor, he has the ability to inspire, instruct, and motivate. His energy, warmth, and humor is making him one of America's dynamic speakers. He is in demand as a conference and keynote speaker, addressing audiences in churches, conferences, corporations, and schools. He has spoken throughout this nation and abroad, speaking throughout Europe, Mexico, and Asia.

He is the author of numerous audio series such as, "Becoming a Person of Excellence", "The Power of Thinking Big,", "Divine Strategies for Success", "Effective Leadership Strategies for the 21st Century", "Increasing your earning potential for wealth", "Divine Strategies for FAMILY Success," and "Stress Free Living" have been distributed worldwide.

Rob lives in Lexington, Ohio along with his wife Tricia (who is expecting twins), daughter Cierra, sons Christian and Grayson, their miniature schnauzer, Tyson.

For additional information, scheduling speaking engagements, or to write the author, please address your correspondence to:

Robert Yanok International

P.O. Box 2635 Mansfield, OH 44906

www.robertyanok.com • e-mail: robertyanok@mac.com

Can I Introduce you to the Source of All Success?

If you have never received Jesus Christ as your personal Lord and Savior, why not do it right now? Simply repeat this prayer with sincerity:

"Lord Jesus, I believe that you are the Son of God. I believe that You became man and died on the cross for my sins. I believe that you were raised from the dead and the Savior of the world. I confess that I am a sinner and I ask you to forgive me, and to cleanse me of all my sins. I accept your forgiveness, and I receive You as my Lord and Savior. In Jesus' Name, I pray. Amen!"

"...if you confess with your mouth, and believe in your heart that God raised him from the dead, you will be saved. For it is with your heart that you believe and are justified, and it is with your mouth that you confess and are saved... for everyone who calls on the name of the Lord will be saved."
- Romans 10:9,10, 13

"If we confess our sins, he is faithful and just and will forgive us our sins and purify us from all unrighteousness."
- I John 1:9

WE WANT TO HEAR FROM YOU!

An old Chinese proverb says that a journey of a thousand miles begins with one step. By deciding to pray this prayer you have just taken the first step toward success. If you prayed this prayer sincerely, call us at 419.524.1212. Also, we want to hear your praise reports and testimonies of God's Success' in your life! Write us at:

ROBERT YANOK II
P.O. Box 2635 Mansfield, OH 44906
www.robertyanok.com • e-mail: robertyanok@mac.com

Remember this, God has wanted to bless you with success from the first day you received Him as your Lord and Savior. He has been waiting for two things to change in your life:

1. Your lifestyle to line up with His Word.
2. Your understanding to increase regarding His principles of biblical economics.

As you have completed this book I pray its truth has blessed and helped you in your spiritual growth and journey to success. In closing, let me show you how this book can help in an even greater dimension.

First, make a list of five people that you want to see increase and become successful in all areas of their lives.

1.
2.
3.
4.
5.

Make a quality decision to give each of them a gift copy of this book. Now let me show you how this strategic move will benefit you even more from this book.

"Knowing that whatsoever good thing any man doeth, the same shall he receive of the Lord, whether he be bond or free."
- EPHESIANS 6:8

This says that as you help these special friends succeed and prosper, God will help you succeed and prosper.

MORE FROM ROBERT YANOK

CD SERIES

Increasing Your Earning Potential For Wealth

CD SERIES

Becoming a Person of Excellence

Robert Yanok

Pardon Me...
Can You
Spare Some
CHANGE ?

TAPE SERIES

Pardon Me, Can you Spare some Change

ORDER ONLINE:

www.robertyanok.com